THE NEW SANDWICH COOKBOOK

DISCOVER THE JOYS OF SANDWICHES WITH DELICIOUS SANDWICH RECIPES IN AN EASY SANDWICH COOKBOOK

By
BookSumo Press
Copyright © by Saxonberg Associates
All rights reserved

Published by
BookSumo Press, a DBA of Saxonberg Associates
http://www.booksumo.com/

ABOUT THE AUTHOR.

BookSumo Press is a publisher of unique, easy, and healthy cookbooks.

Our cookbooks span all topics and all subjects. If you want a deep dive into the possibilities of cooking with any type of ingredient. Then BookSumo Press is your go to place for robust yet simple and delicious cookbooks and recipes. Whether you are looking for great tasting pressure cooker recipes or authentic ethic and cultural food. BookSumo Press has a delicious and easy cookbook for you.

With simple ingredients, and even simpler step-by-step instructions BookSumo cookbooks get everyone in the kitchen chefing delicious meals.

BookSumo is an independent publisher of books operating in the beautiful Garden State (NJ) and our team of chefs and kitchen experts are here to teach, eat, and be merry!

INTRODUCTION

Welcome to *The Effortless Chef Series*! Thank you for taking the time to purchase this cookbook.

Come take a journey into the delights of easy cooking. The point of this cookbook and all BookSumo Press cookbooks is to exemplify the effortless nature of cooking simply.

In this book we focus on Sandwiches. You will find that even though the recipes are simple, the taste of the dishes are quite amazing.

So will you take an adventure in simple cooking? If the answer is yes please consult the table of contents to find the dishes you are most interested in.

Once you are ready, jump right in and start cooking.

— BookSumo Press

TABLE OF CONTENTS

About the Author 2

Introduction 3

Table of Contents 4

Any Issues? Contact Us 7

Legal Notes 8

Common Abbreviations 9

Chapter 1: Easy Sandwich Recipes 10

    Italian Chicken Gyros 10

    Sweet Tuna Sandwiches 12

    Mock Crab Salad Rolls 14

    Holiday Watercress Sandwiches 16

    Homemade Rolls 18

    Smoky Pulled Chicken Lunch Box Sandwiches 20

    Barbeque Chopped Chicken Sandwiches 22

    Asparagus and Egg Sandwich 24

    Parmesan Bacon Sandwiches 27

    Greek Focaccia 29

    Summer Salami Sandwiches 31

    New Hampshire Seafood Salad Sandwiches 33

    Saucy Beef Roast Sandwiches 35

    Easiest French Dip 37

Chicago Inspired Pastrami on Rye 39

How to Make Bread for Sandwiches 41

Downstate Banana Sandwich 43

Spicy Mexicana Sandwiches 45

Backyard Caprese Sandwich 47

College Meatball Parmigiana 49

Cucumber Salad Sandwiches 51

Balsamic Pepper Ciabattas 53

Country Pecan Salad Sandwiches 55

Sweet Turkey Sandwich 57

Vegetarian Gyros 59

Southern Chicken Cutlets with Slaw 61

Southwest Roast Beef Sandwiches 64

Apple and Turkey Sandwiches 66

Artisanal PB Sandwiches 68

Waffle Dessert Sandwich 70

Summer Cucumber Sandwiches 72

Baja Club Sandwich 74

Japanese Teriyaki Rolls 76

Garden Party Chicken Sandwiches 78

Little Beaver Sandwiches 80

Spicy Tilapia Sandwiches 82

Pickle Sandwiches 85

Topped Haddock Sandwiches 87

Buttered Apple Sandwiches 89

Shibuya Salmon Sandwiches ... 91
Italian Turkey Club ... 93
Turkey Muffin Sandwiches ... 95
Upstate Reuben ... 97
Ginger Snap Dessert Sandwiches ... 99

Appendix I: Additional Recipes ... 101
Mango & Raisin Chutney ... 101
Spiced Apple Chutney ... 103
Minty Yogurt Chutney ... 105
Herbed Grape Chutney ... 107
Mixed Veggie Chutney ... 109

THANKS FOR READING! JOIN THE CLUB AND KEEP ON COOKING WITH 6 MORE COOKBOOKS.... ... 111
Come On... ... 113
Let's Be Friends :) ... 113

ANY ISSUES? CONTACT US

If you find that something important to you is missing from this book please contact us at info@booksumo.com.

We will take your concerns into consideration when the 2nd edition of this book is published. And we will keep you updated!

— BookSumo Press

Legal Notes

ALL RIGHTS RESERVED. NO PART OF THIS BOOK MAY BE REPRODUCED OR TRANSMITTED IN ANY FORM OR BY ANY MEANS. PHOTOCOPYING, POSTING ONLINE, AND / OR DIGITAL COPYING IS STRICTLY PROHIBITED UNLESS WRITTEN PERMISSION IS GRANTED BY THE BOOK'S PUBLISHING COMPANY. LIMITED USE OF THE BOOK'S TEXT IS PERMITTED FOR USE IN REVIEWS WRITTEN FOR THE PUBLIC.

COMMON ABBREVIATIONS

cup(s)	C.
tablespoon	tbsp
teaspoon	tsp
ounce	oz.
pound	lb

*All units used are standard American measurements

Chapter 1: Easy Sandwich Recipes

Italian Chicken Gyros

Ingredients

- 1 lb. cooked chicken breast, chopped
- 1/2 C. olive oil
- 1/2 C. tomatoes, chopped
- 4 oz. feta cheese, crumbled
- 2 1/4 oz. sliced pitted olives, drained
- 1 C. lettuce, shredded
- 1 C. Italian salad dressing mix
- 6 pita breads

Directions

- In a bowl, add all ingredients except pita breads and mix until well combined.
- Divide the tomato mixture onto half of each pita bread.
- Fold each pita bread and secure with toothpicks.
- Enjoy.

Servings per Recipe: 6

Timing Information:

| Preparation | 10 mins |
| Total Time | 10 mins |

Nutritional Information:

Calories	377.4
Fat	29.3g
Cholesterol	81.3mg
Sodium	378.2mg
Carbohydrates	2.2g
Protein	25.6g

* Percent Daily Values are based on a 2,000 calorie diet.

Sweet Tuna Sandwiches

Ingredients

- 1 (6 oz.) cans low-sodium tuna in water
- 1 tbsp light mayonnaise
- 1 tsp sweet pickle relish
- 1 tsp Dijon mustard
- 1 stalk celery, chopped
- 1/4 C. diced onion
- 1/4 tsp pepper
- 1/8 tsp celery seed
- 4 slices raisin bread

Directions

- In a bowl, add all the ingredients except bread slices and mix until well combined.
- Refrigerate for about 1 hour.
- Place the tuna mixture onto 2 bread slices evenly.
- Cover with the remaining slices and enjoy.

Servings per Recipe: 2

Timing Information:

| Preparation | 5 mins |
| Total Time | 35 mins |

Nutritional Information:

Calories	283.5
Fat	5.6g
Cholesterol	28.3mg
Sodium	370.6mg
Carbohydrates	31.5g
Protein	26.4g

* Percent Daily Values are based on a 2,000 calorie diet.

Mock Crab Salad Rolls

Ingredients

- 1 (8 oz.) packages imitation crab meat
- 1/2 C. Miracle Whip
- 2 stalks celery, chopped
- 3 tbsp red onions, chopped
- salt and pepper

Optional

- 4 hamburger buns
- 4 large lettuce leaves, washed and dried

Directions

- In a blender, add the crab and process for about 2-3 seconds.
- Add the Miracle Whip and process for about 2 seconds.
- Transfer the crab mixture into a bowl with onion, celery, salt and pepper and mix well.
- Place 1 lettuce leaf onto each roll and top with the crab mixture.
- Enjoy.

Servings per Recipe: 4

Timing Information:

| Preparation | 10 mins |
| Total Time | 10 mins |

Nutritional Information:

Calories	257.4
Fat	8.1g
Cholesterol	19.6mg
Sodium	967.8mg
Carbohydrates	36.3g
Protein	9.1g

* Percent Daily Values are based on a 2,000 calorie diet.

Holiday Watercress Sandwiches

Ingredients

- 6 eggs
- 1/3 C. chives, chopped
- salt
- pepper
- 1/3 C. mayonnaise
- 2 tsp white wine vinegar
- 2 tsp Dijon mustard
- 4 slices bread, toasted
- 1 small bunch watercress

Directions

- In a pan of the water, add the eggs over medium heat and cook, covered until boiling.
- Remove from the heat and keep aside, covered for about 10 minutes.
- Drain the eggs and place into a bowl of the cold water for about 10 minutes.
- After cooling, peel the eggs and then, chop them roughly.
- In a bowl, add the chopped eggs and remaining ingredients except the bread and watercress and gently, stir to combine.
- Place the watercress onto each bread slice evenly and top with the egg mixture.
- Enjoy.

Servings per Recipe: 4

Timing Information:

Preparation	15 mins
Total Time	32 mins

Nutritional Information:

Calories	252.9
Fat	14.6g
Cholesterol	284.0mg
Sodium	401.8mg
Carbohydrates	18.1g
Protein	11.7g

* Percent Daily Values are based on a 2,000 calorie diet.

Homemade Rolls

Ingredients

- 1 1/4 C. water
- 2 tbsp vegetable oil
- 2 tsp sugar
- 1 tsp salt
- 3 -3 1/4 C. bread flour
- 1/3 C. powdered milk
- 1 1/2 tsp yeast

Directions

- In the pan of bread machine, place all the ingredients in order as suggested by the manual.
- Select the Dough cycle and press the Start button.
- After the completion of cycle, place the dough onto a lightly floured surface.
- Make 10-12 balls for the dough and shape each into a roll.
- Arrange the rolls onto a lightly greased baking sheet and keep aside in warm place for about 45-50 minutes.
- Set your oven 375 degrees F.
- Cook in the oven for about 20 minutes.
- Enjoy with your favorite condiments as a sandwich.

Servings per Recipe: 10

Timing Information:

Preparation	10 mins
Total Time	2 hrs. 10 mins

Nutritional Information:

Calories	186.8
Fat	4.2g
Cholesterol	4.1mg
Sodium	250.3mg
Carbohydrates	31.3g
Protein	5.2g

* Percent Daily Values are based on a 2,000 calorie diet.

Smoky Pulled Chicken Lunch Box Sandwiches

Ingredients

- 12 oz. boneless skinless chicken breasts
- 2 C. chicken stock
- 2/3 C. brown sugar
- 1/4 C. tomato sauce
- 1/4 C. minced onion
- 2 minced garlic cloves
- 2 tbsp Worcestershire sauce
- 1 tbsp liquid smoke
- 1/2 tsp hot sauce
- 1/8 tsp cumin
- 3 tbsp grill seasoning
- 1 tbsp flour
- 12 hamburger buns, toasted

Directions

- In a pot, add the stock over medium heat and cook until heated completely.
- Add the chicken and cook for about 4-5 minutes per side.
- With a slotted spoon, transfer the chicken onto a plate; reserve the stock into the same pot.
- Keep the chicken aside to cool.
- For the sauce: in a bowl, add all the remaining ingredients except the flour and buns and mix until well combined.
- Add the sauce mixture into the reserved simmering stock over medium-low heat and cook for about 5 minutes, stirring frequently.
- Meanwhile, with 2 forks, shred the chicken breasts.
- Add the shredded chicken into the pot and stir to combine well.
- Add the flour, stirring continuously until well combined.
- Cook until sauce becomes thick, stirring continuously.
- Place the chicken mixture onto each roll and enjoy.

Servings per Recipe: 8

Timing Information:

| Preparation | 20 mins |
| Total Time | 35 mins |

Nutritional Information:

Calories	329.7
Fat	4.0g
Cholesterol	26.4mg
Sodium	519.4mg
Carbohydrates	54.7g
Protein	17.7g

* Percent Daily Values are based on a 2,000 calorie diet.

Barbeque Chopped Chicken Sandwiches

Ingredients

- 2 whole chickens, cooked, deboned, and chopped
- 1 large onion
- 2 C. water
- 1 1/4 C. ketchup
- 1/4 C. brown sugar
- 1/4 C. Worcestershire sauce
- 1/4 C. red wine vinegar
- 1 tsp salt
- 1 tsp celery seed
- 2 tsp chili powder
- 1/2 tsp hot sauce
- hamburger bun

Directions

- In a crock pot, add all the ingredients except the buns and stir to combine.
- Set the crock pot on Low and cook, covered for about 6-8 hours.
- Place the chicken mixture onto buns and enjoy.

Servings per Recipe: 8

Timing Information:

Preparation	20 mins
Total Time	8 hrs. 20 mins

Nutritional Information:

Calories	802.4
Fat	53.2g
Cholesterol	243.8mg
Sodium	1044.0mg
Carbohydrates	20.0g
Protein	58.2g

* Percent Daily Values are based on a 2,000 calorie diet.

Asparagus and Egg Sandwich

Ingredients

- 8 -10 asparagus spears, washed and trimmed
- 2 tbsp butter, divided
- salt and pepper
- 2 slices pumpernickel bread
- 2 slices Monterey jack cheese
- 1 -2 tbsp thousand island dressing
- 3 slices red onions, cut into rings

Dressing

- 1 1/2 C. mayonnaise
- 1 hard-boiled egg, crushed
- 1 C. ketchup
- 1/4 C. dill relish
- salt and pepper
- lemon pepper

Directions

- For the dressing: in a bowl, add all the ingredients and mix until well combined.
- Transfer in an airtight jar and place in the fridge until using.
- In a pan, add the water and salt and cook until boiling.
- Add the asparagus spears and cook for about 1 minute.
- Drain the asparagus well and immediately, transfer into an ice bath.
- In a skillet, add 1 tbsp of the butter over medium heat and cook until melted.
- Add the asparagus and stir fry for about 1-2 minutes.
- Stir in the salt and pepper and transfer into a bowl.
- Spread the remaining butter onto both bread slices evenly.
- In the same skillet, place the slices, buttered side down and cook until golden brown.
- Flip the bread slices.

- Arrange 1 cheese slice onto each bread slice and cook until cheese melts completely.
- Transfer the slices onto a plate and top each with the dressing.
- Place the asparagus onto 1 slice, followed by the onion rings.
- Cover with the remaining slice.
- Cut sandwich in half and enjoy with a garnishing of the pickle slices.

Servings per Recipe: 1

Timing Information:

| Preparation | 15 mins |
| Total Time | 25 mins |

Nutritional Information:

Calories	2439.4
Fat	172.1g
Cholesterol	418.7mg
Sodium	6959.7mg
Carbohydrates	208.3g
Protein	36.9g

* Percent Daily Values are based on a 2,000 calorie diet.

Parmesan Bacon Sandwiches

Ingredients

- 1/2 bag fresh spinach, chopped
- 1 C. grated Swiss cheese
- 1/2 C. Parmesan cheese
- 1/4-1/2 C. mayonnaise
- 2 tbsp mustard
- 4 -8 slices rye bread
- 4 -8 slices turkey bacon
- butter

Directions

- In a bowl, add the mayonnaise, Parmesan cheese, Swiss cheese, spinach and mustard and mix until combined nicely.
- Place the mayonnaise mixture onto half of the bread slices evenly, followed by the bacon.
- Cover with the remaining bread slices.
- Coat both sides of each sandwich with the butter.
- Heat a skillet and cook the sandwiches until golden brown from both sides.
- Enjoy hot.

Servings per Recipe: 2

Timing Information:

| Preparation | 20 mins |
| Total Time | 20 mins |

Nutritional Information:

Calories	810.8
Fat	54.9g
Cholesterol	110.1mg
Sodium	1662.8mg
Carbohydrates	43.3g
Protein	35.7g

* Percent Daily Values are based on a 2,000 calorie diet.

Greek Focaccia

Ingredients

- 1 focaccia bun, split
- tzatziki, sauce
- 1 slice provolone cheese
- 1 slice cheddar cheese
- 1/4 red pepper, sliced
- 1 slice large tomatoes
- 2 rings large red onions
- 1/4 cucumber, sliced
- 1/2 C. mixed greens

- 1 (6 oz.) containers fat free Greek yogurt
- 1/2 cucumber, seeds removed, grated and squeezed
- 1 tbsp red wine vinegar
- 1 tbsp extra virgin olive oil
- 2 garlic cloves, minced
- 1/2 tsp garlic powder
- salt and pepper

White Sauce

Directions

- For the white sauce: in a bowl, add all the ingredients and stir until well combined.
- Refrigerate overnight.
- Place the white sauce on top half of the bun, followed by the provolone slice.
- Arrange the cheddar slice onto the bottom half of the bun, followed by the remaining ingredients.
- Cover with the top half and cut in half.
- Enjoy.

Servings per Recipe: 1

Timing Information:

Preparation	20 mins
Total Time	20 mins

Nutritional Information:

Calories	698.0
Fat	33.0g
Cholesterol	52.1mg
Sodium	776.0mg
Carbohydrates	69.8g
Protein	33.0g

* Percent Daily Values are based on a 2,000 calorie diet.

Summer Salami Sandwiches

Ingredients

- 2 tsp French mustard
- 8 slices bread, buttered
- 125 g cheddar cheese, sliced
- 12 slices Italian salami
- 2 eggs
- 1 tbsp olive oil
- salt and pepper
- oil

Directions

- Place the mustard onto the buttered side of each bread slice evenly.
- Place the cheese slices onto each of 4 bread slices, followed by the salami.
- Cover with the remaining bread slices and press together strongly.
- In a bowl, add 1 tbsp of the oil, eggs, salt and pepper and beat until well combined.
- Coat each sandwich with the egg mixture evenly.
- In a skillet, add the oil and cook until heated through.
- Add the sandwiches in batches and fry until golden brown from both sides, flipping occasionally.
- Transfer onto paper towel-lined plate to drain.
- Enjoy warm.

Servings per Recipe: 4

Timing Information:

| Preparation | 5 mins |
| Total Time | 15 mins |

Nutritional Information:

Calories	528.3
Fat	35.0g
Cholesterol	181.2mg
Sodium	1374.6mg
Carbohydrates	27.3g
Protein	24.5g

* Percent Daily Values are based on a 2,000 calorie diet.

New Hampshire Seafood Salad Sandwiches

Ingredients

- 1 lb. cooked shrimp, peeled, de-veined and chopped
- 3 hard-boiled eggs, chopped
- 3 celery ribs, minced
- 1/2 C. mayonnaise
- 1 dash onion salt
- salt and pepper
- 1 dash seasoning salt
- 1 dash celery salt
- 8 slices your choice bread, toasted
- lettuce
- tomatoes, slices

Directions

- In a bowl, add the shrimp, mayonnaise, eggs, celery, seasoning salt, salt and pepper and mix until blended nicely.
- Place the extra mayonnaise on both sides of bread.
- Place the shrimp mixture onto bread and top with the lettuce and tomato.
- Cut the sandwiches in half and enjoy.

Servings per Recipe: 1

Timing Information:

Preparation	20 mins
Total Time	20 mins

Nutritional Information:

Calories	445.4
Fat	17.4g
Cholesterol	386.6mg
Sodium	1608.1mg
Carbohydrates	35.3g
Protein	34.8g

* Percent Daily Values are based on a 2,000 calorie diet.

SAUCY BEEF ROAST SANDWICHES

Ingredients

- 1 large onion, sliced
- 1 (14 oz.) cans beef broth
- 4 lb. beef boneless beef rump roast, fat trimmed
- 2 tbsp balsamic vinegar
- 1 (2/3 oz.) envelope Italian salad dressing mix
- 1/2 tsp salt
- 1/4 tsp black pepper
- 12 hoagie rolls, split
- 1 large green bell pepper, sliced
- 12 slices provolone cheese, halved

Directions

- Drizzle the beef roast with the vinegar evenly.
- In a crock pot, add the onion slices and broth and top with the beef roast.
- Sprinkle with the salt, dressing mix and pepper.
- Set the crock pot on Low and cook, covered for about 8-10 hours.
- With a slotted spoon, transfer the beef roast onto a cutting board.
- Cut the roast into thin slices.
- Add the roast slices to the crock pot and mix with the pan mixture completely.
- Place the beef onto the buns, followed by the bell peppers and cheeses.
- Enjoy.

Servings per Recipe: 12

Timing Information:

| Preparation | 15 mins |
| Total Time | 8 hrs. 15 mins |

Nutritional Information:

Calories	277.8
Fat	10.0g
Cholesterol	19.3mg
Sodium	776.8mg
Carbohydrates	32.9g
Protein	13.4g

* Percent Daily Values are based on a 2,000 calorie diet.

Easiest French Dip

Ingredients

- 4 tbsp dry onion soup mix
- 3 C. water
- 2 tsp instant beef bouillon
- 1 lb. sliced deli roast beef
- 4 large hoagie rolls
- 2 tbsp butter
- 2 tbsp horseradish
- salt and pepper

Directions

- In a coffee grinder, add the dry onion soup mix and pulse until fine.
- In a microwave-safe casserole dish, add the instant beef bouillon, dry onion soup mix and water and microwave on High for about 4-5 minutes, mixing once half way through.
- Cover the casserole dish and keep aside.
- Arrange the meat slices onto a microwave-safe plate.
- With a paper towel, cover the plate and microwave on Medium-High for about 1-2 minutes.
- Cut each bun in half lengthwise, leaving a hinge.
- Coat each bun with the butter, followed by the horseradish and beef slices.
- Sprinkle with the salt and pepper and cover with top halves.
- Cut each sandwich in half.
- Place the beef broth mixture into serving bowls.
- Dip each sandwich into broth mixture and enjoy.

Servings per Recipe: 4

Timing Information:

Preparation	4 mins
Total Time	7 mins

Nutritional Information:

Calories	376.2
Fat	12.1g
Cholesterol	69.7mg
Sodium	2265.0mg
Carbohydrates	38.7g
Protein	26.7g

* Percent Daily Values are based on a 2,000 calorie diet.

Chicago Inspired Pastrami on Rye

Ingredients

- 2 lb. cooked and sliced beef pastrami
- 4 -8 slices Havarti cheese
- coarse grind mustard
- dill pickle slices
- sliced onion
- 8 -16 slices artisan rye bread
- 1 C. beef broth

Directions

- In a pan, add the broth and cook until just boiling.
- Add the pastrami and cook until heated through.
- Place the meat onto half of bread slices, followed by the cheese, mustard, pickles and onions.
- Cover with the remaining slices.
- Heat a grill pan and cook the sandwich until golden brown from both sides.
- Enjoy warm.

Servings per Recipe: 4

Timing Information:

Preparation	10 mins
Total Time	20 mins

Nutritional Information:

Calories	595.1
Fat	22.6g
Cholesterol	181.2mg
Sodium	2841.8mg
Carbohydrates	32.2g
Protein	61.8g

* Percent Daily Values are based on a 2,000 calorie diet.

How to Make Bread for Sandwiches

Ingredients

- 3 3/4 C. all-purpose flour
- 2 tsp salt
- 1 C. warm whole milk
- 1/3 C. warm water
- 2 tbsp unsalted butter, melted
- 3 tbsp honey
- 2 1/4 tsp instant yeast
- 1 tbsp butter, softened

Directions

- In a bowl, add the honey, butter, milk, water and yeast and mix until well combined. In the bowl of the stand mixer, add 3 1/2 C. of the flour and salt. Slowly, add the yeast mixture into the flour and beat on medium speed for about 10 minutes.
- Place the dough onto a floured surface and with your hands, knead until a dough ball forms. Place the dough into a greased bowl and turn to coat well. With a plastic wrap, cover the bowl and place in a warm area for about 40-50 minutes.
- Place the dough onto a floured surface and gently, roll into a 1x9-inch rectangle. Roll the short side of the dough rectangle into a tight cylinder. With your hands, pinch the seams closed.
- In the bottom of a greased 9×5-inch loaf pan, arrange the dough, seam-side down. With a plastic wrap, cover the loaf pan and place in a warm area for about 20-30 minutes.
- Set your oven to 350 degrees F. Arrange the loaf pan in a glass baking dish with the boiling water. Cook in the oven for about 40-50 minutes. Remove from the oven and coat the bread with the melted butter. Place the bread onto a wire rack to cool.

Servings per Recipe: 10

Timing Information:

Preparation	1 hr 30 mins
Total Time	2 hrs. 15 mins

Nutritional Information:

Calories	238.1
Fat	4.7g
Cholesterol	11.6mg
Sodium	487.9mg
Carbohydrates	42.5g
Protein	6.0g

* Percent Daily Values are based on a 2,000 calorie diet.

DOWNSTATE BANANA SANDWICH

Ingredients

- 1 whole wheat bagel, toasted
- 2 tbsp reduced-fat cream cheese
- 1/2 banana, mashed
- 2 tsp strawberry preserves

Directions

- In a bowl, add the preserves, cream cheese and banana and mix well.
- Place the banana mixture onto the bagel and enjoy.

Servings per Recipe: 1

Timing Information:

Preparation	5 mins
Total Time	5 mins

Nutritional Information:

Calories	149.3
Fat	4.7g
Cholesterol	16.2mg
Sodium	145.7mg
Carbohydrates	24.9g
Protein	3.0g

* Percent Daily Values are based on a 2,000 calorie diet.

Spicy Mexicana Sandwiches

Ingredients

- 2 jalapeño peppers, halved lengthwise and seeded
- 2 slices sourdough bread
- 1 tbsp butter, softened
- 1 tbsp cream cheese
- 1/4 C. Colby-Monterey jack cheese, shredded
- 1 tbsp tortilla chips, crushed

Directions

- Set the broiler of your oven and arrange the rack in the top shelf of the oven.
- Arrange the peppers onto a baking sheet, cut side down.
- Cook in the oven for about 8-14 minutes.
- Remove from the oven and transfer the peppers into a re-sealable bag.
- Seal and keep aside for about 20 minutes.
- Carefully, remove the skins from the peppers.
- Place the cream cheese onto 1 bread slice evenly, followed by the roasted jalapeño peppers and cheese.
- Cover with the remaining bread slice.
- Place the bread onto both sides of the sandwich and top with the crushed chips.
- Place a skillet over heat and cook until heated.
- Place the sandwich and cook for about 2-3 minutes per side.

Servings per Recipe: 1

Timing Information:

Preparation	34 mins
Total Time	40 mins

Nutritional Information:

Calories	642.7
Fat	27.8g
Cholesterol	71.6mg
Sodium	963.6mg
Carbohydrates	75.9g
Protein	23.3g

* Percent Daily Values are based on a 2,000 calorie diet.

BACKYARD CAPRESE SANDWICH

Ingredients

- 2 rye bread slices, toasted
- 1 medium vine ripe tomato, sliced
- fresh cold iceberg lettuce
- cold dill pickle slices
- any type of sliced cheese
- Miracle Whip
- salt and pepper

Directions

- Place the Miracle Whip onto both bread slices evenly.
- Place 2-3 tomato slices onto 1 bread slice, followed by the lettuce, pickles and cheese.
- Cover with the remaining bread slice.
- Cut into half and enjoy.

Servings per Recipe: 1

Timing Information:

Preparation	5 mins
Total Time	5 mins

Nutritional Information:

Calories	155.1
Fat	1.8g
Cholesterol	0.0mg
Sodium	261.6mg
Carbohydrates	30.0g
Protein	4.9g

* Percent Daily Values are based on a 2,000 calorie diet.

College Meatball Parmigiana

Ingredients

- 1 lb. lean ground beef
- 6 Ritz crackers, crushed
- 1/4 C. Parmesan cheese, grated
- 3/4 C. spaghetti sauce, divided
- 12 cheddar cheese cubes
- 4 hot dog buns

Directions

- Set your oven to 400 degrees F before doing anything else and grease a shallow baking dish.
- In a bowl, add the beef, Parmesan cheese, cracker crumbs and 1/4 C. of the spaghetti sauce and mix until well combined.
- Make 12 equal sized meatballs from the mixture.
- In the bottom of the prepared baking dish, arrange the meatballs about 2-inch apart.
- Place 1 cheese cube on top of each meatball and press into center deeply.
- Cook in the oven for about 15 minutes.
- Meanwhile, in a microwave-safe bowl, add the remaining spaghetti sauce and microwave on High for about 30 seconds.
- Spread the sauce onto each bun evenly.
- Place 3 meatballs into each bun and enjoy.

Servings per Recipe: 1

Timing Information:

Preparation	10 mins
Total Time	25 mins

Nutritional Information:

Calories	597.2
Fat	33.6g
Cholesterol	133.2mg
Sodium	835.1mg
Carbohydrates	28.6g
Protein	42.6g

* Percent Daily Values are based on a 2,000 calorie diet.

Cucumber Salad Sandwiches

Ingredients

- 2 (8 oz.) packages cream cheese, softened
- 3/4 C. mayonnaise
- 3 C. diced cooked chicken
- 3/4 C. peeled seeded and diced cucumber
- 3 celery ribs, diced
- 1/2 C. red bell pepper, diced
- 6 green onions, chopped small
- 1 tsp garlic salt
- 1/2 tsp salt
- 1/2 tsp ground black pepper
- 84 slices fresh white bread, crust removed

Directions

- In a bowl, add the mayonnaise and cream cheese and mix until combined nicely.
- Add the remaining ingredients except the bread slices and mix until well combined.
- Cover the bowl and refrigerate for about 12-24 hours.
- With a medium-sized cookie cutter, cut the bread slices into desired shapes.
- Place the chicken mixture onto half of the bread pieces evenly.
- Cover with the remaining pieces and enjoy.

Servings per Recipe: 1

Timing Information:

| Preparation | 30 mins |
| Total Time | 30 mins |

Nutritional Information:

Calories	114.8
Fat	4.1g
Cholesterol	11.4mg
Sodium	200.4mg
Carbohydrates	15.2g
Protein	3.9g

* Percent Daily Values are based on a 2,000 calorie diet.

Balsamic Pepper Ciabattas

Ingredients

- 4 large red bell peppers
- 2 tbsp olive oil
- 1 tbsp balsamic vinegar
- 2 garlic cloves, minced
- 2 tsp kosher salt
- 1 tsp ground black pepper
- 2 tbsp capers, drained
- 1 large ciabatta, halved horizontally
- 1 (11 oz.) garlic and herb goat cheese
- 8 -10 large basil leaves
- 3 slices red onions
- kosher salt
- ground black pepper

Directions

- Set your oven to 500 degrees F before doing anything else.
- Arrange the whole peppers onto a baking sheet pan in a single layer.
- Cook in the oven for about 30-40 minutes, flipping two times.
- Remove the baking sheet from the oven and immediately with a piece of foil, cover it tightly. Keep aside for about 30 minutes.
- Meanwhile, in a bowl, add the garlic, vinegar, oil, salt and pepper and beat until well combined. Remove the foil and cut each pepper in quarter. Carefully, remove the peel and seeds of each pepper.
- In a bowl, add the peppers with any accumulate juices, the oil mixture and capers and mix well. With a plastic wrap, cover the bowl and place in the fridge for about 2-3 hours.
- Place the goat cheese onto bottom half of the loaf, followed by the peppers, basil and onions rings.
- Season with the salt and pepper and cover with the top half of the loaf.
- Cut into desired sized pieces and enjoy.

Servings per Recipe: 4

Timing Information:

Preparation	10 mins
Total Time	50 mins

Nutritional Information:

Calories	124.0
Fat	7.3g
Cholesterol	0.0mg
Sodium	1008.1mg
Carbohydrates	12.7g
Protein	2.1g

* Percent Daily Values are based on a 2,000 calorie diet.

COUNTRY PECAN SALAD SANDWICHES

Ingredients

- 3 large carrots, shredded
- 2/3 C. pecans, ground
- 1 garlic clove, minced
- 4 stuffed green olives, minced
- mayonnaise
- 8 bread slices

Directions

- In a bowl, add the green olives, carrots, garlic pecans and enough mayonnaise and mix until a moistened mixture is formed.
- Place a thin layer of mayonnaise onto 4 bread slices, followed by the carrot mixture.
- Cover with the remaining bread slice.
- Cut each sandwich in half and enjoy.

Servings per Recipe: 4

Timing Information:

Preparation	10 mins
Total Time	20 mins

Nutritional Information:

Calories	148.8
Fat	13.2g
Cholesterol	0.0mg
Sodium	37.3mg
Carbohydrates	7.9g
Protein	2.2g

* Percent Daily Values are based on a 2,000 calorie diet.

SWEET TURKEY SANDWICH

Ingredients

- 2 slices bread, Italian
- 2 tbsp mayonnaise
- 1 tomatoes, cut into four slices
- 1/4 tsp salt
- 1/4 tsp pepper, ground black
- 1 tbsp basil, sliced
- 3 slices turkey, oven roasted
- 2 slices cheese, provolone
- 1 tbsp mango chutney, see appendix
- 1 tbsp butter

Directions

- Sprinkle the tomato slices with the salt and pepper evenly.
- Place the mayonnaise onto 2 bread slices evenly.
- Place the tomato slices onto 1 bread slice, followed by the basil, turkey slices, mango chutney and cheese slices.
- Cover with the remaining bread slice.
- Spread a thin layer of butter on both sides of the sandwich.
- Heat a skillet and cook the sandwich and cook until golden brown from both sides.

Servings per Recipe: 1

Timing Information:

Preparation	5 mins
Total Time	10 mins

Nutritional Information:

Calories	749.6
Fat	51.0g
Cholesterol	110.8mg
Sodium	2251.0mg
Carbohydrates	47.0g
Protein	27.7g

* Percent Daily Values are based on a 2,000 calorie diet.

Vegetarian Gyros

Ingredients

Sauce

- 1 C. low-fat plain yogurt
- 2 tbsp tahini
- 1 garlic clove
- 1 tsp lemon juice
- salt

Pita

- 4 large whole wheat pita bread

- 8 oz. feta cheese
- 4 tomatoes, plum, ripe and diced
- 1 C. spinach leaves, torn into pieces
- 1 C. alfalfa sprout
- 1 large avocado, ripe, halved, pitted, peeled and cut into wedges
- 1 cucumber, diced

Directions

- For the sauce: in a bowl, add all the ingredients and mix until well combined.
- Carefully, cut an edge from each pita bread to open the pockets.
- In another bowl, add the spinach, tomatoes, feta and 1/4 C. of the sauce and gently, toss to coat.
- Place the spinach mixture into each pita pocket.
- Arrange 1 pita pocket onto each serving plate.
- Place the avocado, cucumber and sprouts around each pita pocket evenly.
- Enjoy with a drizzling of the remaining sauce.

Servings per Recipe: 4

Timing Information:

Preparation	20 mins
Total Time	20 mins

Nutritional Information:

Calories	545.4
Fat	28.2g
Cholesterol	57.2mg
Sodium	1079.2mg
Carbohydrates	57.3g
Protein	22.7g

* Percent Daily Values are based on a 2,000 calorie diet.

Southern Chicken Cutlets with Slaw

Ingredients

- 4 boneless skinless chicken breasts
- kosher salt
- 1 quart buttermilk

Dressing

- 1 tbsp Dijon mustard
- 3 tbsp red wine vinegar
- 1 tsp kosher salt
- 1/2 C. extra virgin olive oil

Slaw

- 1 small red onion, sliced
- 1 C. red wine vinegar
- 2 jalapeños, seeded, cut in half and sliced crosswise
- 1/4 C. parsley, chopped
- 1/2 green cabbage, core and outer leaves removed, and sliced
- kosher salt

Breading

- 1 lb. all-purpose flour
- 1 tbsp cayenne pepper
- 1 tbsp kosher salt
- 1 1/2 tsp ground pepper
- 2 quarts vegetable oil
- 4 rolls, sliced lengthwise

Directions

- Sprinkle the salt over each chicken breast evenly and keep aside for about 6-8 minutes.
- In a casserole dish, place the buttermilk and chicken breasts and place in the fridge for all night.
- For the vinaigrette: in a bowl, add all the ingredients except the oil and mix well.
- Slowly, add oil, beating continuously until well combined.

- For the coleslaw: in a bowl, add the vinegar and onions and keep aside for about 25 minutes.
- Drain the onions, discarding the vinegar.
- In a bowl, add the cabbage, onions, parsley, jalapeño, salt and vinaigrette and toss to coat well.
- In a shallow bowl, add the flour, salt, cayenne and pepper and mix well.
- Remove the chicken breasts from the buttermilk and let the excess drip off.
- Coat each chicken breast with the flour mixture evenly, then dip into buttermilk and finally, coat with the flour mixture.
- In a deep skillet, add the oil and cook until its temperature reaches to 365 degrees F.
- Add the chicken breasts and cook for about 1 minute without stirring.
- Now, fry the chicken breasts for about 5-7 minutes.
- With a slotted spoon, transfer the chicken breasts onto paper towels-lined plate to drain.
- Immediately, sprinkle the chicken breasts with the salt.
- Arrange 1 chicken breast on bottom half of each roll, followed by the coleslaw.
- Cover with the top half and enjoy.

Servings per Recipe: 4

Timing Information:

| Preparation | 1 hr 30 mins |
| Total Time | 1 hr 45 mins |

Nutritional Information:

Calories	4967.6
Fat	472.3g
Cholesterol	85.3mg
Sodium	2959.4mg
Carbohydrates	139.1g
Protein	52.8g

* Percent Daily Values are based on a 2,000 calorie diet.

Southwest Roast Beef Sandwiches

Ingredients

- 4 oz. diced green chilies, drained
- 1/2 C. mayonnaise
- 1/2 lb. deli roast beef, sliced
- 1/4 lb. Swiss cheese, sliced
- 8 slices sourdough bread
- margarine

Directions

- In a bowl, add the green chilies and mayonnaise and mix well.
- Spread the butter onto one side of each bread slice evenly.
- Now, place the mayonnaise mixture onto another side of each bread slice evenly.
- Place a nonstick skillet over medium heat until heated through.
- Place 4 slices in the skillet, butter side down and top each with 1 cheese slice, roast slices and a second cheese slice.
- Cover with the remaining bread slices, buttered side up.
- Cook until golden brown from both sides.
- Enjoy hot.

Servings per Recipe: 4

Timing Information:

Preparation	15 mins
Total Time	15 mins

Nutritional Information:

Calories	664.7
Fat	22.0g
Cholesterol	60.9mg
Sodium	1888.4mg
Carbohydrates	83.7g
Protein	33.3g

* Percent Daily Values are based on a 2,000 calorie diet.

APPLE AND TURKEY SANDWICHES

Ingredients

- 1 C. cooked turkey, cubed
- 1/2 C. celery, diced
- 1 small Red Delicious apple, cored and cubed
- 2 tbsp walnuts, chopped
- 1 tbsp reduced-calorie mayonnaise
- 1 tbsp plain fat-free yogurt
- 1/8 tsp nutmeg
- 1/8 tsp cinnamon
- 4 lettuce leaves
- 8 slices raisin bread

Directions

- In a bowl, add the yogurt, mayonnaise, turkey, apple, celery, walnuts, cinnamon and nutmeg and mix until well combined.
- Cover the bowl and place in the fridge 8-12 hours.
- Place 1 lettuce leaf onto each of 4 bread slices, followed by the turkey mixture.
- Cover with the remaining bread slices and enjoy.

Servings per Recipe: 4

Timing Information:

Preparation	15 mins
Total Time	1 hr 15 mins

Nutritional Information:

Calories	259.9
Fat	7.7g
Cholesterol	27.9mg
Sodium	277.3mg
Carbohydrates	33.1g
Protein	15.6g

* Percent Daily Values are based on a 2,000 calorie diet.

ARTISANAL PB SANDWICHES

Ingredients

- 2 slices bread, toasted
- 8 tsp peanut butter
- fruit sliced

Directions

- Place the peanut butter onto both bread slices evenly.
- Place fruit slices over each bread slices and enjoy.

Servings per Recipe: 2

Timing Information:

Preparation	3 mins
Total Time	6 mins

Nutritional Information:

Calories	194.4
Fat	11.7g
Cholesterol	0.0mg
Sodium	270.1mg
Carbohydrates	16.9g
Protein	7.3g

* Percent Daily Values are based on a 2,000 calorie diet.

Waffle Dessert Sandwich

Ingredients

- 2 toasted hot waffles
- 1 C. ice cream

Toppings

- 1-2 tbsp decorative candies
- 1-2 tbsp crushed nuts
- 1-2 tbsp toasted coconut
- 1-2 tbsp granola cereal
- 1-2 tbsp praline
- peanut butter spread on before ice cream

Directions

- Place a thin layer of the peanut butter onto one waffle, followed by the ice cream and your favorite garnishing.
- Cover with the remaining waffle and roll it.
- Enjoy.

Servings per Recipe: 1

Timing Information:

Preparation	5 mins
Total Time	7 mins

Nutritional Information:

Calories	709.7
Fat	35.6g
Cholesterol	161.5mg
Sodium	872.1mg
Carbohydrates	80.5g
Protein	16.4g

* Percent Daily Values are based on a 2,000 calorie diet.

Summer Cucumber Sandwiches

Ingredients

- 1/4 C. sour cream
- 1 (3 oz.) packages cream cheese, softened
- 2 tsp dill weed, chopped
- 1 tsp lemon juice
- 12 slices rye cocktail bread
- 1 medium cucumber, sliced
- 6 slices smoked salmon, halved crosswise
- grated lemon peel
- dill sprig

Directions

- In a bowl, add the cream cheese, sour cream, lemon juice and dill weed and mix until well combined.
- Refrigerate for about 2 hours.
- Place the cream cheese mixture onto each bread slice evenly, followed by cucumber slices and salmon.
- Enjoy with a garnishing of the fresh dill and lemon peel.

Servings per Recipe: 6

Timing Information:

Preparation	15 mins
Total Time	1 hr 15 mins

Nutritional Information:

Calories	110.9
Fat	7.2g
Cholesterol	20.6mg
Sodium	146.7mg
Carbohydrates	9.5g
Protein	2.5g

* Percent Daily Values are based on a 2,000 calorie diet.

Baja Club Sandwich

Ingredients

- 1 loaf unsliced round bread, halved horizontally
- 1 C. bottled sour cream and bacon salad dressing
- lettuce
- 1/3 lb. sliced Swiss cheese
- 3/4 lb. sliced cooked roast beef
- 1/2 lb. sliced cooked turkey
- 1 large tomatoes, sliced

Directions

- Carefully, hollow out the center of each bread half, leaving about 1/4-inch shell.
- Place about 1/3 C. of the sour cream into each bread shell, followed by the bacon dressing.
- Place half of the lettuce into the bottom of each shell, followed by the cheese, roast beef, remaining dressing, turkey, tomato and remaining lettuce.
- Cover each with the top shell.
- Cut into desired sized wedges and enjoy.

Servings per Recipe: 6

Timing Information:

| Preparation | 10 mins |
| Total Time | 10 mins |

Nutritional Information:

Calories	446.0
Fat	15.8g
Cholesterol	96.1mg
Sodium	448.2mg
Carbohydrates	36.2g
Protein	38.4g

* Percent Daily Values are based on a 2,000 calorie diet.

Japanese Teriyaki Rolls

Ingredients

- 1/2 C. oil
- 1/4 C. soy sauce
- 3 tbsp honey
- 2 tbsp white wine vinegar
- 1 tsp ginger
- 3/4 tsp garlic powder
- 4 boneless skinless chicken breast halves
- 4 hard rolls
- 1 C. shredded lettuce, to serve
- 8 slices tomatoes
- 4 green pepper rings
- 1/4 C. mayonnaise

Directions

- In a bowl, add the oil, soy sauce, honey, vinegar, and ginger and garlic powder and mix until blended nicely.
- Transfer 1/4 C. of the honey mixture into a bowl and reserve in fridge.
- Add the chicken breasts into the bowl with the remaining honey mixture and mix well.
- Place in the fridge overnight.
- Set the broiler of your oven.
- Remove the chicken breasts from the bowl and discard the marinade.
- Cook the chicken under the broiler until desired doneness.
- Place the lettuce onto the bottom half of each roll, followed by the tomato, chicken and green pepper.
- Top each with the reserved honey mixture, followed by the mayonnaise.
- Cover with the top roll and enjoy.

Servings per Recipe: 4

Timing Information:

| Preparation | 10 mins |
| Total Time | 45 mins |

Nutritional Information:

Calories	615.0
Fat	32.9g
Cholesterol	75.5mg
Sodium	1458.3mg
Carbohydrates	47.0g
Protein	33.3g

* Percent Daily Values are based on a 2,000 calorie diet.

Garden Party Chicken Sandwiches

Ingredients

- 4 slices chicken breasts
- 2 crusty buns, halved
- 1 tbsp garlic powder
- 4 tbsp butter
- 1/2 tsp parsley
- sliced tomatoes
- cut up lettuce
- mayonnaise
- sliced black olives
- salt

Directions

- Set the broiler of your oven.
- In a bowl, add the butter, parsley and garlic powder and mix well.
- Place the butter mixture onto the crusty buns evenly.
- Cook the buns under the broiler for about 2 minutes.
- Transfer the buns onto a platter.
- Place the chicken onto he bottom half of each bun, followed by the tomatoes, lettuce, olives and mayonnaise.
- Cover each with top half and enjoy warm.

Servings per Recipe: 2

Timing Information:

| Preparation | 8 mins |
| Total Time | 10 mins |

Nutritional Information:

Calories	339.7
Fat	24.9g
Cholesterol	61.0mg
Sodium	411.8mg
Carbohydrates	24.8g
Protein	5.1g

* Percent Daily Values are based on a 2,000 calorie diet.

LITTLE BEAVER SANDWICHES

Ingredients

- 1 C. applesauce
- 8 slices bread
- 1/4 C. butter, softened
- 1 tbsp sugar
- 1/4 tsp ground cinnamon

Directions

- Place the applesauce onto 4 bread slices and cover with the remaining slices.'
- Place the butter on the outsides of each sandwich.
- Heat a skillet over medium-high heat and cook the sandwiches for about 3-4 minutes per side
- Meanwhile, in a bowl, add the cinnamon and sugar and mix.
- Enjoy the sandwiches hot with a dusting of the cinnamon sugar.

Servings per Recipe: 4

Timing Information:

Preparation	10 mins
Total Time	26 mins

Nutritional Information:

Calories	295.7
Fat	13.2g
Cholesterol	30.5mg
Sodium	374.7mg
Carbohydrates	41.2g
Protein	4.0g

* Percent Daily Values are based on a 2,000 calorie diet.

Spicy Tilapia Sandwiches

Ingredients

- vegetable oil
- 1/2-3/4 lb. fresh tilapia fillets, washed and pat dried
- 3/4 tbsp Cajun seasoning
- 3/4 C. all-purpose flour
- 3/4 C. panko breadcrumbs
- 1 egg
- 1 tbsp Dijon mustard
- 1 1/2 tbsp water
- 2 mini baguette, lightly toasted
- 4 slices tomatoes
- 4 green lettuce leaves
- 4 thin slices red onions

Mayo

- 2 tbsp mayonnaise
- 1 tbsp lemon juice
- 1 - 1 1/2 tbsp Frank's hot sauce
- 1/2 tsp rice vinegar

Directions

- For the spicy Mayonnaise: in a bowl, add the mayonnaise, rice vinegar, hot sauce and lemon juice and mix until well combined.
- Season the both sides of the fish fillets with Cajun seasoning lightly.
- In a shallow bowl, mix together the flour ad 1 1/2 tbsp of the Cajun seasoning.
- In a second shallow bowl, add the Dijon mustard, egg and 1 1/2 tbs. of the water and beat well.
- In a third shallow bowl, add the breadcrumbs.
- Coat the fish fillets with the flour mixture, then dip in the egg mixture and finally, coat with the breadcrumbs.
- In a skillet, add the oil and cook until heated through.
- Add the fish fillets and fry for about 5-6 minutes.
- With a slotted spoon, transfer the fish fillets onto a paper towel-lined plate to drain.

- Place the spicy mayonnaise onto the inner sides of the baguettes evenly, followed by the fish fillets, romaine, tomatoes and onion slices.
- Enjoy.

Servings per Recipe: 2

Timing Information:

Preparation	20 mins
Total Time	25 mins

Nutritional Information:

Calories	3601.8
Fat	31.2g
Cholesterol	153.5mg
Sodium	6045.6mg
Carbohydrates	671.0g
Protein	160.4g

* Percent Daily Values are based on a 2,000 calorie diet.

PICKLE SANDWICHES

Ingredients

- 2 slices whole wheat bread
- 1-2 slice cheddar cheese
- 1-3 tbsp butter, softened
- 1-2 kosher dill pickle
- 1-2 sliced Vidalia onion

Directions

- Place the remaining butter on both bread slices evenly.
- In a skillet, add 1 tbsp of the butter over medium heat and cook until melted.
- Place 1 bread slice, buttered side down and top with 1-2 cheese slices, followed by the pickle and onion slices.
- Cover with the remaining bread slice, buttered side up.
- Cook until golden brown from both sides.
- Enjoy hot.

Servings per Recipe: 1

Timing Information:

Preparation	5 mins
Total Time	12 mins

Nutritional Information:

Calories	410.3
Fat	23.3g
Cholesterol	59.9mg
Sodium	1387.3mg
Carbohydrates	39.9g
Protein	13.9g

* Percent Daily Values are based on a 2,000 calorie diet.

TOPPED HADDOCK SANDWICHES

Ingredients

- 2 tbsp low-fat mayonnaise
- 2 tbsp nonfat plain yogurt
- 2 tsp rice vinegar
- 1/8-1/4 tsp crushed red pepper flakes
- 8 oz. canned pineapple chunks, drained and chopped
- 2 C. coleslaw mix
- 1/4 C. cornmeal
- 1 1/4 lb. haddock, skinned and cut into 4 portions
- 1/2 tsp Cajun seasoning
- 1/4 tsp salt
- 4 tsp canola oil, divided
- 8 slices whole wheat bread, toasted

Directions

- In a bowl, add the yogurt, mayonnaise, vinegar and red pepper flakes and beat until well combined.
- Add the coleslaw mix and pineapple and gently, stir to coat.
- In a shallow bowl, place the cornmeal.
- Season the haddock pieces with the Cajun seasoning and salt evenly and then, coat with the cornmeal.
- In a nonstick skillet, add 2 tsp of the oil over medium-high heat and cook until heated through.
- Add 2 haddock pieces and cook for about 4 minutes, flipping once half way through.
- Transfer the haddock pieces onto a plate.
- Repeat with the remaining 2 tsp of the oil and haddock pieces.
- Place the haddock pieces onto each of 4 bread slices, followed by the pineapple mixture.
- Cover with the remaining bread slice and enjoy.

Servings per Recipe: 4

Timing Information:

Preparation	15 mins
Total Time	25 mins

Nutritional Information:

Calories	365.2
Fat	7.5g
Cholesterol	93.6mg
Sodium	794.9mg
Carbohydrates	36.5g
Protein	37.3g

* Percent Daily Values are based on a 2,000 calorie diet.

BUTTERED APPLE SANDWICHES

Ingredients

- 2 slices cinnamon raisin bread
- 1 slice American cheese
- 1/4 small apple, sliced
- 2 tsp butter, softened

Directions

- Place the cheese slice onto 1 bread slice, followed by apple slices.
- Top with the remaining bread slice.
- Place the butter onto both sides of the sandwich evenly.
- Heat a skillet over medium heat and cook the sandwich for about 2 minute per side.

Servings per Recipe: 1

Timing Information:

| Preparation | 10 mins |
| Total Time | 10 mins |

Nutritional Information:

Calories	293.8
Fat	15.1g
Cholesterol	33.7mg
Sodium	462.4mg
Carbohydrates	32.6g
Protein	8.4g

* Percent Daily Values are based on a 2,000 calorie diet.

Shibuya Salmon Sandwiches

Ingredients

- 1 (6 oz.) cans salmon
- 4 oz. cream cheese
- 1 avocado, peeled, pitted and sliced
- 1 tbsp lemon juice
- 2 tsp wasabi powder
- 2 tsp soy sauce
- 2 tsp rice vinegar
- 1 tsp sesame seeds
- 4 rice cakes
- pickled ginger

Directions

- In a bowl, add the tuna, salmon and lemon juice and with a fork, flake to combine.
- Add the cream cheese, soy sauce and wasabi and mix until blended nicely.
- Place the fish mixture onto each rice cake evenly, followed by the avocado slices and sesame seeds.
- Drizzle with the rice vinegar and a little soy sauce.
- Top with the pickled ginger and enjoy.

Servings per Recipe: 2

Timing Information:

Preparation	5 mins
Total Time	5 mins

Nutritional Information:

Calories	546.4
Fat	39.1g
Cholesterol	101.5mg
Sodium	647.1mg
Carbohydrates	26.7g
Protein	25.2g

* Percent Daily Values are based on a 2,000 calorie diet.

Italian Turkey Club

Ingredients

- 1 loaf focaccia bread, halved horizontally
- 1 (3 1/2 oz.) jars prepared pesto sauce
- 1/2 lb. sliced black forest ham, optional
- 1/2 lb. sliced roasted turkey breast
- 6 slices provolone cheese
- 1/2 small red onion, sliced

Directions

- Set your oven to 450 degrees F before doing anything else.
- Place the pesto onto the cut sides of bread evenly.
- Place the ham onto the bottom half of bread, followed by the turkey, cheese and onion evenly.
- Top with the remaining bread half.
- With a piece of the foil, cover the bread and cook in the oven for about 10 minutes.
- Cut into 6 equal sized wedges and enjoy.

Servings per Recipe: 6

Timing Information:

Preparation	10 mins
Total Time	20 mins

Nutritional Information:

Calories	221.7
Fat	13.3g
Cholesterol	65.4mg
Sodium	761.1mg
Carbohydrates	2.6g
Protein	21.7g

* Percent Daily Values are based on a 2,000 calorie diet.

TURKEY MUFFIN SANDWICHES

Ingredients

- 1 dinner roll, muffin
- mayonnaise
- 1 -2 slice deli turkey
- 1 slice cheese

Directions

- Cut out a cylindrical-shaped piece from the muffin by inserting the knife in the bottom piercing towards the top.
- Slightly thin the walls by pinching them from the inside.
- Fill the muffin with some turkey, followed by the cheese and more turkey meat.
- Trim a small part of the muffin cylinder and insert it back into its place in the bread.

Servings per Recipe: 1

Timing Information:

Preparation	5 mins
Total Time	5 mins

Nutritional Information:

Calories	297.2
Fat	16.3g
Cholesterol	52.9mg
Sodium	1022.9mg
Carbohydrates	19.9g
Protein	17.7g

* Percent Daily Values are based on a 2,000 calorie diet.

Upstate Reuben

Ingredients

- 4 tbsp thousand island dressing, divided
- 3/4 C. sauerkraut
- 8 slices dark pumpernickel bread
- 1 tsp caraway seed
- 4 slices Swiss cheese
- 8 oz. turkey breast
- cooking spray

Directions

- Place the dressing on one side of all bread slices.
- Place the turkey breast onto 4 slices, followed by the sauerkraut, caraway seeds and cheese.
- Cover with the remaining bread slices.
- Place a lightly greased nonstick skillet over medium-high heat until heated through.
- Place the sandwiches and cook for about 1 minute.
- Flip the sandwiches and spray the top with the cooking spray.
- Cook for about 1 minute.
- Remove from the heat and keep aside to cool slightly.
- Cut in half and enjoy.

Servings per Recipe: 4

Timing Information:

Preparation	10 mins
Total Time	20 mins

Nutritional Information:

Calories	421.4
Fat	19.4g
Cholesterol	66.7mg
Sodium	830.8mg
Carbohydrates	35.6g
Protein	26.0g

* Percent Daily Values are based on a 2,000 calorie diet.

GINGER SNAP DESSERT SANDWICHES

Ingredients

- 10 oz. lemon curd
- 8 oz. cream cheese, softened
- 32 ginger snaps

Directions

- In a bowl, add the cream cheese and lemon curd and mix until smooth.
- Place the curd mixture onto ginger cookies evenly.
- Top with remaining cookies and enjoy.

Servings per Recipe: 16

Timing Information:

Preparation	15 mins
Total Time	15 mins

Nutritional Information:

Calories	107.7
Fat	6.3g
Cholesterol	15.5mg
Sodium	133.5mg
Carbohydrates	11.1g
Protein	1.8g

* Percent Daily Values are based on a 2,000 calorie diet.

Appendix I: Additional Recipes

Mango & Raisin Chutney

Ingredients

- 1 kg very firm mango
- 2 C. sugar
- 625 ml vinegar
- 1 (5 cm) pieces ginger, peeled
- 4 cloves garlic, peeled
- 2 -4 tsps chili powder
- 4 tsps mustard seeds
- 8 tsps salt
- 1 C. raisins or 1 C. sultana

Directions

- Peel the mango and then remove the pit and chop it.
- In a pan, add sugar and vinegar, leaving about 20ml and simmer, stirring occasionally for about 10 minutes.
- Meanwhile in a food processor, add remaining vinegar, garlic and ginger and pulse till a paste forms.
- Transfer the paste into a pan and simmer, stirring continuously for about 10 minutes.
- Stir in the mango and remaining ingredients and simmer, stirring occasionally for about 25 minutes or till desired thickness of chutney. Transfer the chutney into hot sterilized jars and seal tightly and keep aside to cool.
- This chutney can be stored in dark place for about 1 year but remember to refrigerate after opening.

Amount per serving: 1

Timing Information:

Preparation	20 mins
Total Time	1 hr 5 mins

Nutritional Information:

Calories	627.2
Fat	2.1g
Cholesterol	0.0mg
Sodium	3748.7mg
Carbohydrates	153.4g
Protein	4.2g

* Percent Daily Values are based on a 2,000 calorie diet.

Spiced Apple Chutney

Ingredients

- 2 quarts chopped cored, pared tart apples
- 2 lbs raisins
- 1 C. chopped onion
- 1 C. chopped sweet red pepper
- 4 C. brown sugar
- 3 tbsps mustard seeds
- 2 tbsps ground ginger
- 2 tsps ground allspice
- 2 tsps salt
- 2 hot red peppers
- 1 garlic clove, crushed
- 1 quart vinegar

Directions

- In a pan, mix together all the ingredients and simmer, stirring occasionally for about 1 hour and 15 minutes or till desired thickness of chutney.
- Transfer the chutney into hot sterilized jars and seal tightly and place in a large bowl of boiling water for about 10 minutes.
- (If you like mild flavored chutney than you can add 4 additional C. of apples).

Amount per serving: 10

Timing Information:

Preparation	1 hr
Total Time	2 hrs 15 mins

Nutritional Information:

Calories	708.1
Fat	1.7g
Cholesterol	0.0mg
Sodium	514.7mg
Carbohydrates	177.1g
Protein	4.5g

* Percent Daily Values are based on a 2,000 calorie diet.

Minty Yogurt Chutney

Ingredients

- 6 tbsps plain yogurt
- 1/2 tsp salt
- 2 tsps dried mint
- 1/2 tsp chili powder

Directions

- In a large bowl, mix together all the ingredients and mix till well combined.
- Refrigerate to chill for at least 15 minutes before serving.

Amount per serving: 4

Timing Information:

| Preparation | 3 mins |
| Total Time | 18 mins |

Nutritional Information:

Calories	15.7
Fat	0.8g
Cholesterol	2.9mg
Sodium	305.3mg
Carbohydrates	1.3g
Protein	0.8g

* Percent Daily Values are based on a 2,000 calorie diet.

HERBED GRAPE CHUTNEY

Ingredients

- 4 C. red seedless grapes
- 1 tbsp butter
- 1/2 C. chopped red onion
- 1 tsp fresh rosemary, snipped
- 1/4 tsp dried oregano, crumbled
- 2 tbsps balsamic vinegar

Directions

- Melt butter in a large skillet and sauté the onion for about 5 minutes.
- Stir in the rosemary and oregano and sauté for about 1 minute.
- Meanwhile in a food processor, add the grapes and pulse till chopped roughly.
- Stir in the vinegar and chopped grapes and cook for about 1-2 minutes or till heated completely.

Amount per serving: 1

Timing Information:

| Preparation | 10 mins |
| Total Time | 20 mins |

Nutritional Information:

Calories	24.1
Fat	0.5g
Cholesterol	1.2mg
Sodium	4.0mg
Carbohydrates	5.1g
Protein	0.2g

* Percent Daily Values are based on a 2,000 calorie diet.

Mixed Veggie Chutney

Ingredients

- 1/2 C. white vinegar
- 1 tbsp sugar
- 1 small cucumber, chopped
- 1 small red bell pepper, chopped
- 1 tbsp of fresh mint, chopped
- 1 tbsp lime juice
- 1 small onion, quartered & thinly sliced

Directions

- In a bowl, add sugar and vinegar and stir to combine.
- Add the remaining ingredients and stir till well combined.
- Serve warm or chill after refrigerating. (Before using, remove from refrigerator and keep aside to return to room temperature).

Amount per serving: 8

Timing Information:

Preparation	10 mins
Total Time	10 mins

Nutritional Information:

Calories	21.7
Fat	0.0g
Cholesterol	0.0mg
Sodium	2.2mg
Carbohydrates	4.7g
Protein	0.4g

* Percent Daily Values are based on a 2,000 calorie diet.

Thanks for Reading! Join the Club and Keep on Cooking with 6 More Cookbooks....

http://bit.ly/1TdrStv

To grab the box sets simply follow the link mentioned above, or tap one of book covers.

This will take you to a page where you can simply enter your email address and a PDF version of the box sets will be emailed to you.

Hope you are ready for some serious cooking!

http://bit.ly/1TdrStv

Come On...
Let's Be Friends :)

We adore our readers and love connecting with them socially.

Like BookSumo on Facebook and let's get social!

Facebook

And also check out the BookSumo Cooking Blog.

Food Lover Blog